Learn How to Start a Profitable
Sign / Vinyl Graphics Business

From Home With Less Than
£500 Capital

Martin Woodward

ISBN: 978-1-291-49118-0

Copyright © Martin Woodward - 2012

All rights reserved

Contents

Introduction **5**

Equipment **9**

Coral Draw Explained (in brief) **12**
    Stretching & Condensing *12*
    Curved Lettering *13*
    Contouring *14*
    Outline Lettering *15*
    Shadows *15*
    Welding *15*
    Converting to Curves *16*

Creating PDF Files **17**

Acquiring Graphics **18**
    Importing Graphics to Corel Draw *19*

Sign Application Materials **20**
    Vinyl Coated Magnetic Rubber *20*
    Foamex *21*
    Styrene *22*
    Acrylic (Perspex) *22*
    Corex *23*
    PVC Banner material *23*
    Wheel covers *24*
    Beware of chemicals *24*
    Removing Vinyl Lettering *24*

Vinyl Cutting vs. Digi Printing vs. Screen Printing **26**
    Vinyl Cutting *26*
    'Digi' Printing *27*
    Screen Printing *28*

Making Your First Sign with a Vinyl Cutter **30**

Pricing **40**

Keeping Your Overheads Low **42**
    Keep Impeccable Accounts *42*
    Remain a Sole Trader & Work from Home *43*
    Keep borrowing to the absolute minimum *44*
    Avoid bad debts *44*

Advertising **45**
    Word of Mouth *45*
    Your own Signs *45*
    Yellow Pages *46*
    Direct Mail *46*
    Trade Magazines *46*
    Trade Exhibitions *47*
    Shop Premises *47*
    Car Boot Sales/ Sunday Markets *48*
    Special Interest Magazines *48*
    Special Interest Exhibitions *48*
    Website *49*
    Google Adwords *51*
    Video *51*
    Online Auction Sites *52*
    Brochures/Price Lists *53*

Income Tax **58**
    VAT *59*

Useful Contacts **61**

Introduction

This guide has not been written by someone simply trying to cash in on writing guides about anything they think that they can sell. I have started and run two sign businesses from scratch with minimal capital (from home), built them both up to very profitable businesses and sold them on.

The first business I started in 1982 long before all the modern day computer equipment and software was available. When I started this first business the only way to letter signs was to:

- Sign write them the old conventional way;
- Screen print them (which required expensive artwork and other set up costs); or
- Cut the letters out of acrylic etc, which required hugely expensive equipment.

As I had no sign writing skills, I had to pay other people to produce work for me using a combination of all of the above. Obviously, paying other people to do this work cut into my profit tremendously, but fortunately in the early 80's the Gerber Graphix 2 & 4 plotters came on the market which revolutionised the whole industry.

These were the forerunners of all the incredible machines that are available today although they were very limited. The Graphix 2 would only cut lettering up to 2" high and each individual font required had to be purchased separately at the cost of about £200 each. The machines themselves cost about £4000 for the 2" and £8000 for the 4". Also the vinyl was only available from Spandex as this was perforated to fit the sprockets on the machines.

But with the business that I was generating it was still profitable for me to buy one of these machines along with a small selection of fonts.

Today we are much more fortunate as there are cutters available that can be used via your PC which are far more powerful than the historic Gerbers and can be purchased brand new for as little as £300 or less. Even these entry level machines will cut lettering and graphics up to 600mm high by as long as you want in any font that you can install on your PC. This means that it's quite possible to start a profitable sign business with less than £500 capital. And as the modern machines don't have sprockets; low cost vinyls are widely available from a variety of suppliers.

The potential for generating business with these machines is limitless. I guarantee that you couldn't walk into even a small village without seeing some form of sign that has been produced this way, not to mention the millions of road and vehicle signs!

These machines will also cut vehicle graphics as shown throughout this guide. Producing these alone offers a huge potential for profit from millions of potential customers.

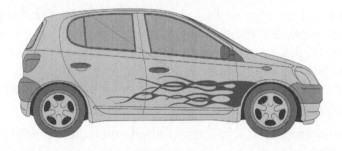

In brief this guide will show you:

- Which machine and accessories to buy and where to get them;
- Where to obtain vinyls and other materials necessary;
- How to get started with Corel Draw;
- Where to get free and/or very low cost graphics;
- How to weed unwanted material;
- How to apply the cut material to your chosen surface;

- How to price your work for maximum profit;
- Different ways of generating business;
- How to keep your overheads low for maximum 'net' profit;
- Effective Advertising;
- Income Tax & VAT;
- Sample Signs;
- Sample Price Guide;
- Plus more.

I also have created two sample websites exclusively for this guide; one dedicated to business signs and the other for vehicle graphics (flames etc.).

These show many samples of what can be achieved easily with a low cost vinyl plotter/cutter as well as a good guide to pricing and designing a suitable website.

These sites can be viewed at:

- http://www.martinwoodward.net/ukmagsigns and
- http://www.martinwoodward.net/locologos

And when you add the possibilities of 'wall art' which can also be created exactly the same way - infinity takes on a new meaning! As an example see http://www.ambiance-live.com/en .

But note that *some* of the items in this site are produced using a digi printer, but many can be created with a standard vinyl cutter.

Equipment

To start with you will need a fairly up to date computer with at least 512MB of Ram. These are so widely available and you've probably got one anyway so we are not going to go into this here.

The only other main item that you will require is a vinyl plotter/cutter. There are a variety of these on the market, but as an entry level easily available on e-bay for about £300 brand new I recommend the Creation P Cut 600. These are available from Sign Wizard who also sell various add on items that you may require and offer good after sales service. Alternatively Premier Signs offer a complete low cost starter package including vinyls.

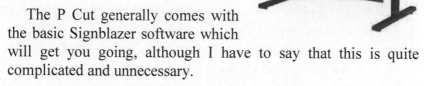

The P Cut generally comes with the basic Signblazer software which will get you going, although I have to say that this is quite complicated and unnecessary.

I recommend that you produce your artwork in Corel Draw for the following reasons:

    a) It's an extremely powerful programme giving you all the features needed for basic sign making;

    b) You can easily produce PDF files to be e-mailed or faxed to your clients as 'proofs'. I'll show you how to do this later;

    c) It's far easier than most of the dedicated sign making software that I've seen;

    d) Corel 12 (or 11) which I recommend can be purchased very economically.

Other items that you will need are:

- Vinyl & application tape;

- As much graphic software as you can obtain;
- A one metre (or more) steel rule;
- A squeegee;
- A large cutting mat;
- A scalpel and cutting knives;
- A pair of pointed tweezers;
- A suitable work environment (I've only ever worked from home);
- Ideally you will also need some very basic accounts software with which to keep your accounts. Excel is fine which you've probably got anyway.

Depending on which market you are aiming at, you may also need a media to apply your lettering/graphics to, but we'll deal with this later.

Vinyl and application tapes are available from a variety of suppliers, so shop around for the best prices. You may find that it's best to buy vinyls from one supplier and other supplies from another. A list of suppliers is shown at the end of the guide.

I would recommend that you start with a small quantity (10 metres each) of about 10 different colours (medium quality) and a few different widths of application tape. As you progress and depending on which direction you want your business to go, you will know which colours/qualities you will need to purchase in greater quantities.

I assure you that I am not receiving and 'backhanders' from any suppliers who are recommended here, so you can be sure that the recommendations are purely on credit and with your best interest in mind!

Before buying a machine (or supplies), look into all the possibilities. Obviously ebay is a good place to start looking, but be sure to download a few brochures, so that you have a better idea about what you are looking for. And don't make the mistake of buying direct from China or Hong Kong where you will be liable for import duties, expensive carriage costs and will have no after sales service.

If buying second-hand or if you fancy splashing out, I would recommend the Roland Camm 24" width (there are various models). The advantage of the Roland is that they are top quality and very easy to use although more expensive than the models recommended above. Expect to pay far more for a second-hand Roland than for a new P Cut (but if you can find one it's worth it).

Recently in Cyprus I used a Roland Stika SX15, which many would consider as nothing more than a 'toy', but it worked well although it would only cut lettering/graphics up to 15" in height (in one go) and was also limited for length. If space is really a problem for you or perhaps you only want to operate part time, then one of these could be a good option. The Stika is also very easy to use and set up and comes with idiot proof software.

The difference between a 'cutter' and a 'plotter' which I'm often asked, is that a cutter is a plotter that 'cuts'! Some plotters are just used for drawing large plans and graphics etc.

Coral Draw Explained (in brief)

Corel Draw is an extremely powerful piece of software. I am completely self-taught at this and as such I am unable to explain it in detail. But I can show you the main aspects of the programme in relation to sign making, which took me months to learn and will save you a deal of pain.

The main reason for using Corel Draw (or any other Sign making software) is that it gives you the ability to manipulate lettering/graphics to a tremendous degree.

All the information here comes from Corel Draw 12. Later versions are basically the same, but with a few new advanced features. Corel 12 (or 11) of course can be purchased one heck of a lot cheaper than later versions and from the sign making point of view will do everything you want.

Stretching & Condensing

The most basic manipulation that you will need is the ability to stretch or condense lettering. The examples below are the same size font (Ariel), one condensed, the other extended.

In order to do this:
- a) Create a text box (the same way as you do in 'Word');
- b) Type in the selected lettering & change fonts as required;
- c) Right click to change it to 'convert to artistic text' and simply drag the text in or out. - Eazzie pezzie!

This can also be done vertically as well as horizontally.

By using the 'interactive envelope' tool (found in the toolbar, or in the effects section) you can create the following effects, simply by dragging from the appropriate points. Have a play!

Curved Lettering

There will be many occasions when you will need to use curved lettering. To do this above a curve is simple, as follows:

a) Firstly you need to create an ellipse or circle the size that you want your lettering to follow;

b) Create your lettering in the font and size that you want. (It's a good idea to copy this so that you can do it again easily if the size is wrong);

c) Click on the 'text' tool and 'fit text to path', then move the arrow to the ellipse, right click and your lettering will follow the curve;

d) Use the 'vertical placement' tool (which will have popped up) to move the lettering above the ellipse. This will then enable you to delete the ellipse (if required) and retain the lettering.

Making a curve underneath an ellipse is a little bit more complicated (although there may be a simpler way that I haven't discovered yet):

a) Firstly you need to create an ellipse as before;

b) Create a rectangle a bit bigger than the ellipse and place the ellipse partially inside the

rectangle as shown;

c) Click on 'arrange' and open 'shaping' and 'trim';

d) Trim the ellipse from the rectangle as shown;

e) Finally, 'fit text to path' as before to create the final result.

This is incidentally simpler in Corel X3 and later.

Contouring

Contouring is an effect that you will need on a regular basis. This enables you to put a different colour around an item of lettering or graphic. To do this:

a) Click on 'effects', then 'contour' and 'outside';

b) Alter the 'offset' according to how large you want the contour to be, then click on the item and apply;

c) By clicking the small centre box at the top, you can alter the colour of the contour with the right hand colour tab;

d) Click 'view' and 'wireframe' and you'll see how the item will be cut out.

You can also put a contour around a contour to produce another effect that you will need regularly. To do this, proceed as previously then:

a) Click on the edge of the contour, right click and 'break contour apart' (you may have to zoom in very close to do this);

b) Put another contour around the contour and again 'break the contour apart';

c) Then go to 'arrange', 'shaping' and 'trim';

d) Click on the inner contour, and click 'trim';

e) Click on the outer contour;

f) Drag the inner contour away and delete;

g) Go to 'view' and 'wireframe' to see how the cutter will cut.

If you've ever seen Coronation Street, you may notice that the 'Cafe' on Roy's window is cut this way!

Outline Lettering

There are several fonts that have an 'outline' option and these can be cut as per the font. But you can create this effect with any font by contouring on the inside, breaking the contour apart and then trimming the inside. Simply adding a black border won't work, which can be seen by viewing the wireframe.

Shadows

A few fonts are naturally 'shadowed', but you can create this effect with any font simply by copying the item, dragging one of them slightly offset and then trimming. Of course you can offset the shadow right, left, above or below as you require. When applying the vinyl, you can either leave a slight gap or take it tight as you wish. Even using just the shadow on its own can create quite a nice effect!

Welding

It's often necessary to 'weld' items together. On the surface this seems unnecessary as the result looks exactly the same in Corel Draw, but when you come to cut the item on your plotter, if not welded, it will cut them as three separate items, creating cut lines where you don't want them.

In order to create and cut a 'bullet' shape;

a) Create an ellipse and a rectangle;

b) Trim the unwanted portion out;

c) Weld the remaining two pieces together.

Converting to Curves

Converting to curves is necessary for a number of purposes. Once an item of lettering or shape has been converted to curves it becomes a graphic and no longer part of a font or basic shape. This (apart from other things) would enable you to send it to someone who didn't have the particular font installed and they would still see it exactly as you sent it.

This also enables you to change the shape of any letter or shape to create interesting effects. This is achieved by double clicking on the item and then dragging the appropriate letter part in or out etc. New drag marks (nodes) can be created by clicking anywhere along the line.

To convert to curves, simply right click on the item and click on the highlight 'convert to curves.'

Creating PDF Files

Why do you need PDF files? - For at least two reasons.

As with converting to curves, PDF files (if set accordingly) are then no longer reliant on the selected fonts being installed. This enables you to create artwork in any size you like and then send 'proofs' (by fax or e-mail) in A4 size to your clients even though they may not have Corel Draw or the selected fonts installed. It also enables you to produce a brochure in Corel Draw and again fax or e-mail it to your clients or include it as an instant download in your website.

To produce a PDF file, click on 'File', then 'Publish to PDF..... Done! Eazzie Pezzie!

But just to make sure, check the following:

a) Click 'file' and 'publish to PDF';

b) Click 'settings' then 'objects';

c) Make sure that 'embed font in document' is checked, or 'export all text as curves'.

This will probably be set as default, but it's not a bad idea to occasionally look at this.

This guide was created in a combination of Corel Draw 12 and MS Word and then converted to PDF.

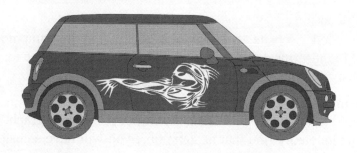

Acquiring Graphics

In order to enhance your work you will need to build a collection of graphics. Many of these can be downloaded free of charge from the internet, although you will almost certainly need to buy some as well.

An easy way to acquire free graphics is to download as many dingbat files as you can, then convert them to curves and save them into categories.

Some of these are really good (especially for 'wall art') and of course they can be manipulated to meet your needs. Shown here are a few randomly taken from the 'poptics extra' font all of which can be cut and/or manipulated easily. Multi coloured graphics can be achieved by cutting each colour separately.

A good website for downloading corporate graphics is www.brandsoftheworld.com and www.simplythebest.net for free dingbats/fonts.

It must be made clear that a plotter will only cut a 'line graphic' (.ai or .eps) or a font; it will not cut a photograph. You will undoubtedly find that at some time you will have a customer who needs a graphic reproducing that is impossible to cut on a plotter. To get round this, you will need to farm this part of the job out to someone who has digi printing equipment. If you make enquiries you'll find that you can get this done very cheaply making it totally unnecessary to invest in hugely expensive equipment (and space and mess).

Importing Graphics to Corel Draw

Once you have acquired some .eps or .ai graphics make sure that you categorise these in itemised document folders so that you know where to find them. Then when you want to import them into to Corel Draw, this is how you do it:

- Click 'file' then 'import';
- Navigate to the appropriate folder;
- Select the correct 'files of type' at the bottom of the page. For .ai files select 'AI', but for .eps files select 'PS, PRN, EPS' and NOT 'EPS' – don't ask me why – it's a mystery!

This last bit of advice should enable you to retain your hair for much longer than me. It took me weeks of pain and misery to figure this out!

Sign Application Materials

Most vinyl lettering/graphics can be applied directly onto windows or vehicles etc., or any other smooth non greasy surface. If you try applying them to a rough surface like a brick wall, they'll just drop off!

No doubt you could generate business just supplying pre spaced lettering/graphics on application tape ready for your clients to apply to the surface of their choice.

However, if you plan on doing business with most trades you will need to look into at least the most common sign materials.

Vinyl Coated Magnetic Rubber

This is my personal favourite product and in my opinion the best product for using with a home run business as it's so easy to work with. Other qualities include:

- Easy to cut with a 'Stanley' knife (but watch your fingers);
- Easy to store and doesn't take up too much room;
- Economical to purchase and very profitable;
- As popular as ever with small businesses.

The main benefits are that it can be applied and removed instantly without doing any damage to the vehicle, enabling the vehicle to be used for personal or business use. Whereas applying (permanent) vinyl lettering directly to any vehicle will cause at least some damage (when removed) and in some cases can even cause the need for a re-spray.

It's important to note that the only thickness that is suitable for vehicle use is the 0.85mm (0.75mm magnetic with .1mm vinyl). The 0.5mm or 0.6mm is no good for this purpose whatsoever (but ideal for fridge magnets).

You can buy magnetic rubber in complete rolls 61cm x 30m (2' x 100') or any length you like off the roll. The best UK supplier by far is Abel Magnets Sheffield (they can deliver nationwide and are most helpful).

Note that magnetic signs will not stick to glass, plastic or aluminium (Smart Cars and Land Rovers) etc. I know this may seem obvious to you, but you'd be amazed at how many clients aren't fully aware of this. I once had a bus company order £2000 worth of signs to use on aluminium bus panels. Fortunately I managed to avert a disaster.

Foamex

This is commonly used for rigid signs and 'A' boards, although it is also suitable for fabricating. The most commonly used thicknesses are 3mm or 5mm. Other attributes are as follows:

- It's extremely durable and very pliable (although it becomes more brittle with age);
- Can be drilled easily and cut with a jigsaw;
- The 3mm can even be cut with a 'Stanley' knife (using a few cuts);
- Is generally UV resistant (but check);
- Fairly low cost;
- Not suitable for illuminating.

Styrene

Similar to Foamex, Styrene is commonly used for rigid signs and 'A' boards, and suitable for fabricating and vacuum forming. The most commonly used thicknesses are 3mm or 5mm. Other attributes are as follows:

- It's extremely durable and very pliable (although it becomes more brittle with age);
- It can be drilled easily and cut with a jigsaw. The 3mm can again be cut with a 'Stanley' knife (using a few cuts);
- Can be fabricated or vacuum formed;
- As against Foamex this *is* suitable for illuminating;
- Most types but not all are UV resistant;
- Fairly low cost.

Acrylic (Perspex)

This is the most expensive and best quality of the commonly used materials. It has a high gloss finish and looks good even after long usage. For small signage the most commonly used thicknesses are again 3mm and 5mm. Other attributes are as follows:

- Very brittle and will shatter if dropped or hit with something hard. However the thicker it is the stronger it is (and the more expensive);

- Ideal for illuminated signs;
- Can be fabricated or vacuum formed;
- Can be drilled carefully and cut with a jigsaw;
- UV resistant;
- Available in a variety of colours;
- Generally expensive.

Corex

This is commonly used by estate agents for their 'For Sale' boards and looks like plastic fluted cardboard. Other attributes are as follows:

- Only suitable for flat signs (cannot be curved or vacuum formed, but can be folded);
- Available in various thicknesses, 3mm and 5mm are the most common;
- Totally waterproof and fairly durable;
- Can be nailed or screwed and easily cut with a 'Stanley' knife;
- Very lightweight;
- Generally UV resistant (but check);
- Very low cost and ideal for a number of low cost and particularly temporary uses.

All of the above plastic materials are best purchased from a local sheet plastics merchant (see Yellow Pages). Expect to pay more if you want them cut to size. Also check sign suppliers such as Spandex.

PVC Banner material

Obviously used for banners, but note that more flexible (and expensive) vinyls could be required. Banners are available in a variety of thicknesses, widths, qualities and prices. If you are considering working with banners, you may struggle with space if working from home. Personally, I've left these alone.

Wheel covers

These are available in rigid or flexible form, the rigid type being very expensive. If using the flexible type, as with the banners, you may need to use a more flexible vinyl. Avoid the flexible ones until you know what you are doing!

To be honest I found places where I could buy these cheaper already printed, rather than the blanks.

Beware of chemicals

With all of the above and any other plastics that you may use, beware of chemicals. Discuss with your local plastic merchant which chemicals can be used for cleaning etc. I can tell you from personal experience that 'petrol' based cleaners will often cause your sign material to 'dissolve' before your eyes. Trust me, I've done it and paid the price! Be warned!

Removing Vinyl Lettering

Most permanent vinyl lettering can be removed with the aid of a hair dryer, and the glue underneath with a glue remover. 'Bettaware' sticky stuff remover is *generally* ok, but do remember that all chemicals react differently on various surfaces. Where ever possible avoid the use of chemicals.

I would also advise you against getting involved in removing lettering from vehicles etc. as it nearly always leaves marks and sometimes damage to the paintwork (unless removed very soon after initial application). This is why I prefer the magnetic material and always warn customers of this possibility.

Vinyl Cutting vs. Digi Printing vs. Screen Printing

Even though you may only be using the vinyl cutting method, it's still important that you understand the advantages and disadvantages of other printing/sign making methods. In all methods, the artwork can be created in Corel Draw (or similar). If using another printing method would be more economical for a client, I would always tell them, thus gaining their trust and respect. Most clients are unaware of the different methods and would initially often go to the wrong place for a quotation.

Some larger operatives may use all three methods, but even then they would not have an advantage over the small operative as their overhead costs would be much higher.

Ok, so let's look at the advantages and disadvantages of each method.

Vinyl Cutting

This is by far the most economical in terms of equipment and 'setting up' costs. Advantages include:

- Superb top quality results and ideal for low quantity runs and 'one off' signs;
- Multicoloured results can be achieved by applying each colour separately;
- Can be applied to most surfaces;
- Vinyl can be removed and altered if required, i.e. if producing a 'take away' price list board - the prices can be changed easily;
- Lettering and/or graphics can be cut and then sent by post if necessary for clients to apply as required;

- Only a small amount of clean equipment is required making it ideal to work from home or a very small business or shop premises;
- Can produce high profits with little effort for very enjoyable work.

Disadvantages are:

- Not suitable for producing photographic images;
- Not economical for long runs.

'Digi' Printing

This is often confused with vinyl cutting as the machines look somewhat similar and the digi printers can also cut in a similar way. So whereas the vinyl cutter simply 'cuts', the digi printer prints *and* cuts. Advantages include:

- Ideal for low quantity runs and 'one off' signs;
- Can produce everything that a vinyl cutter can do plus more;
- Ideal for multicoloured photographic images which can easily be reproduced in one step (including vehicle body wraps);
- Less stock of vinyl required, as all the colours are produced via pigment inks (printed onto clear or white vinyl);
- Can produce multicoloured vinyl stickers and automatically cut them to shape.

Disadvantages are:

- The machines are generally much larger and more messy due to the inks and therefore less suitable for home use, however, Roland do produce a fairly small one;
- Machine and set up costs are much, much more expensive;

- Any printed work cannot be altered after printing;
- If you don't use good quality artwork and a high resolution, the quality can be very poor.

I have to say that had I continued in the business in Cyprus, I probably would have eventually invested in a small digi printer.

Screen Printing

This method requires high set up costs (artwork then screen production) and is extremely messy making it very difficult to work from home. Basic equipment can be purchased fairly inexpensively, but to get serious you would need a large investment.

Advantages are:

- Ideal for long runs, the longer the run the more economical it becomes;
- Multicoloured results can be achieved by applying each colour separately (using a carousel).

Disadvantages are:

- Not suitable for producing photographic images;
- Not suitable for small runs due to high set up costs;
- Extremely messy, not really suitable for operating from home unless in a separate dedicated building/outhouse.

In all cases remember that rather than turning work away that is not suitable for vinyl cutting, get to know some local digi printers and screen printers and farm the work out to them for a commission. Then you can get the benefit of their expensive equipment without the burden of their overheads. I've done this on numerous occasions!

The next page contains a few samples of actual signs that I produced in Cyprus, all of which were created using Corel Draw, cut with a Roland Stika SX15 and applied to a variety of surfaces. Note that all of these examples could alternatively be digi printed of screen printed (but of course would have different set up costs as explained).

Making Your First Sign with a Vinyl Cutter

Firstly familiarise yourself with your equipment. As all cutters are different I can't give specific details here. But basically you need to make sure that your cutter and computer are in communication with one another otherwise nothing will happen. Common initial setup faults are incorrect COMM settings or Baud settings. The COMM settings in your computer are altered via 'device manager' in the control panel and must be the same as the sign cutter's driver software (probably comm. 3 or 4). But if all else fails - READ THE MANUAL!

You will also obviously need to feed some vinyl into the cutter, but again the manual will show you how to do this.

Most cutters will have settings for cutting speed and pressure. I recommend that you choose a fairly slow speed to start with, and then increase it as you gain confidence.

The pressure required is determined by the material used and is achieved by trial and error. Basically if the pressure is too deep you will cut right through the material and the backing sheet. If the pressure is not deep enough, the material will not cut deep enough to weed out the waste. Experiment by cutting just one letter at a time - it's not rocket science! Also make sure that you always keep a spare blade (or two). Sod's law dictates that they always break at the worst possible time!

Now having got the machine set up correctly we're ready to cut our first sign. We'll start with something simple where you won't waste too much material and apply it to a window and then remove it afterwards.

Either in Corel Draw or the basic sign machine software type in the words: 'Hello Mum!' about 50mm high and pick a font without serifs.

Notice the difference between the three H's; one rounded with no serifs, one with square serifs and one with pointed serifs. (*Now you know what a serif is!*) Without doubt the pointed serif 'Times New Roman' is the most difficult to weed particularly on small lettering, and this is why I've chosen 'Ariel rounded' to begin with. Another good rounded font is 'Vag'.

It makes no difference which colour you use, but as we are going to stick it on a window, yellow or white will stand out best. I've used yellow because it will be easier for you to see what you are doing when it comes to 'weeding', although white is actually best for windows.

As we are going to stick the result onto the inside of a window we need to 'mirror' the image. In Corel Draw this is achieved by clicking the 'arrange' button then 'transformation' then 'mirror and 'apply'.

Next we need to make it a bit easier to weed off the sheet so you need to draw a box around your lettering. You can do this for the whole line or for each letter as you choose. Some software enables you to put a horizontal cut through the middle but without cutting the lettering. This makes weeding a 'breeze'

Your result so far should look like the image below. Then let the cutter do its work.

Having cut your vinyl you will then need to weed out the unwanted material, which is best done with a scalpel and/or pointed tweezers. When you first do this you will probably get into a fair mess, but after only a little practice you will be doing it like lightening.

You should then be left with the image to the right all nicely weeded out.

Now you are ready for applying the application tape. To start with you'd probably be best now cutting your work off the roll of vinyl and taking it to a smooth flat surface (kitchen work-top if the wife's not around), then apply the application tape trying to avoid wrinkles (but don't worry if you get a few, it's not that important).

Then run a credit card or plastic scraper over this to increase the adhesion. You can get special 'squeegees' tailor made for this purpose (many vinyl suppliers will give them out free).

Before removing the backing paper, mark the centre of the application tape as a guide which will help you in the next step.

Gently remove the backing paper so that the vinyl is stuck in reverse only onto the application tape. I find it best to turn it upside down to do this and gently peel the backing paper off. Again, practice makes perfect. It won't take you long to get good at it.

Finally you need to apply the vinyl to the application surface (the window) which can be done either wet or dry.

Dry application is as follows:

    a) Using a removable marker or crayon, draw a level line where you want the bottom of the lettering to be, and another mark where the centre of the lettering should be;

    b) Carefully offer the vinyl (on the application tape) onto the surface, lining up the centre mark on the application tape with the mark on the window, be careful not to let any part actually touch until you know everything is aligned correctly;

c) Smooth it down with the scraper, gently remove the application tape then wipe out the marking lines - Voila!

But with this method you have to get it positioned correctly first time. To be honest I did it this way for years and am pretty good at it, but it is much easier applying it wet.

Wet application is as follows:

a) Mark the window as before, but this time you need to use a marker that is both removable and waterproof. Depending on the surface, I use either crayon, masking tape or nothing;

b) Spray a soapy solution (about the same consistency as you'd use for washing dishes, if you've never washed any dishes ask your mother) onto the application surface. Get plenty on, and then apply the vinyl (still obviously on the application tape) which can then be moved around or even re-lifted as required;

c) When positioned correctly, smooth out the water bubbles with the scraper and wait until the vinyl has dried onto the surface, this could take between half an hour and a day depending on how much soap you used and the application material. If using the magnetic material, it dries pretty quickly, but onto a window or especially Corex it will take a little longer. You can speed the process up with a hair drier if you want to;

d) When the material is dry, gently remove the application tape to finish!

Note that during this process, don't worry if you damage one or more letters, these can be re-cut and applied the same way later.

For two or more colours you need to do one colour at a time, which is why you need to charge more for extra colours.

Now as an alternative to the above result, you could weed out the opposite way to produce the result as shown below. But if you use this method and make a mistake with the lettering you'd have to start again.

Using a combination of both 'positive' and negative' lettering you can create some interesting signs with only one colour as shown here.

I think you'll agree that these signs give a two colour feel, while only using one colour! More similar designs as well as multicoloured examples are shown in the dedicated website http://www.martinwoodward.net/ukmagsigns.

Feel free to copy these if you wish.

Another problem that you might have is transferring your work from Corel Draw to your cutter.

Many cutters will simply cut direct, but if you have a problem it can be solved in one of two ways:

    a) Firstly you could export your work to an eps file and then your cutter should accept it. To do this; simply go to 'file' then 'export' then choose eps (2nd on the list).

    b) Alternatively you could use another program to do this. We found a programme called Sign Cut X2 which as a standalone programme is useless, but to transfer from Corel it's perfect. It also has some great weeding functions. The only downside is that you will probably have to buy it, but you can try it free first. You will find this at http://www.sc-x2.com. After installing this you will need to click on the 'application launcher' icon in Corel Draw (in the top tool bar).

Finally, before your wife comes home, you'd better get that lettering off your window. This can easily be peeled off but to get the adhesive off you will need to either pinch some of your wife's nail polish remover or get some 'sticky stuff remover'. As mentioned previously (you can also buy this in most DIY stores).

You will find a video example of fitting graphics to a vehicle in both of the dedicated websites and if you search You Tube no doubt you will find many more of these.

Ok, so that's dealt with your first bit of cutting and applying, which I hope has been explained clearly. Now we'll move on to something slightly more complicated which is going to be a four colour graphic of 'Hong Kong Phooey' as shown here.

Now if you look closely you'll see that there are five colours:

- Black (outline);
- Orange (coat);
- Skin colour;
- Grey (nose/ears);

- Yellow (belt).

Now the colours that you'll actually use will be determined by which colour vinyls you have in stock, but we'll assume that you have some that are reasonably suitable. You may have noted that I said 'four' colours but there are actually five. Well this is because *I'm* going to give Hong Kong Phooey a *black* belt which I think he deserves!

So this is how we do it:

a) Firstly you need to right click on the graphic and 'ungroup all';

b) If like me you want to give him a black belt you will need to remove the inner belt shape otherwise the cutter will cut round this shape. Just simply drag it out and delete it. If you think he only deserves a yellow belt then ignore this;

c) Allow the cutter to cut out the full graphic in black;

d) Weed out all the inside to leave the black outline as shown here. You can apply the application tape to this graphic now or later;

e) Then move onto the grey colour for his nose and ears. As there is only a small amount of this if you don't want to waste a load of vinyl it's best to copy the full graphic and then delete everything except for the nose and ears on one of these. Then cut these out in grey. You could just leave these bits in black if you wish (drag and delete as with the belt);

f) Repeat this for his orange coat to leave the graphic as shown below;

g) If you've decided to give him a miserable yellow belt, then repeat again for this;

h) Now because his skin colour covers virtually all of the graphic, you might as well cut the whole lot out in the correct colour and then weed out everything except what is needed as shown again below;

i) If you haven't already done so apply the application tape to each section;

j) Starting with the outline, apply each section to your chosen surface. Obviously you will have to wait for each bit to dry before removing the application tape, but remember you could use a hair dryer if you are in a hurry.

Voila! We have our finished product complete with black belt and looking ready for action!

I have assumed here that this is being applied to a white background. If not, you will also have to cut the white band on his coat as an additional step.

Part 2

GENERATING BUSINESS

Pricing

Basically anyone can buy a plotter and some vinyl and knock a few signs together. But turning it into profit is where most people fail. This section deals with: pricing; overheads; advertising and Tax & VAT. If you follow the advice detailed here there's absolutely no reason why you shouldn't end up with a successful profitable business.

One of the first things that you have to get right is 'pricing'. People who've not been in business before often make the mistake of thinking that if they bought something for £1.00 and sold it for £2.00 they've made a profit. Not so!

Many years ago before I started my first sign business (although I was self employed at the time anyway) I bought a small book called 'The Lazy Man's Way to Riches'. If you are lucky enough to ever see this publication, I urge you to grab a copy.

One of the best bits of advice in this book is: if you don't get a 3 - 1 mark up at the very least - forget it! 5 - 1 or 10 - 1 or more is more sensible. But in the case of sign making, you have to take into account: all your material costs (vinyl; application tape; application media) AND your time.

It's not unreasonable to expect your overheads to be 50% of your turnover (although this can be reduced if you remain a sole trader working from home and keep good accounts). Following are a few calculations showing how different mark ups can affect your net profit. Obviously these are hypothetical, but interesting nonetheless. It's also worth noting that the further you keep your turnover away from the VAT threshold the less grief you will have.

5 - 1 Mark Up		10 - 1 Mark Up		10 - 1 Mark Up	
Turnover	£ 50,000.00	Turnover	£ 50,000.00	Turnover	£ 30,000.00
Materials	£ 10,000.00	Materials	£ 5,000.00	Materials	£ 3,000.00
Overheads	£ 25,000.00	Overheads	£ 25,000.00	Overheads	£ 15,000.00
Net Profit	**£ 15,000.00**	**Net Profit**	**£ 20,000.00**	**Net Profit**	**£ 12,000.00**

With the last sign business that I started in Cyprus (working alone from home) I worked out my prices at between an 8 - 1 (minimum) and 25 - 1 (where possible) mark up and achieved results similar to this last calculation on a part time basis.

Actual	
Turnover	£ 20,000.00
Materials	£ 3,000.00
Overheads	£ 2,000.00
Net Profit	**£ 15,000.00**

The dedicated websites that I've created for this book will also give you a good idea about pricing, but of course material costs are constantly changing and vary according to location, so you must continually monitor your prices and delivery costs (where applicable). More about this later.

Keeping Your Overheads Low

Remember that your overheads come off your profit, and not just off your turnover. You could have a high turnover and a high 'gross' profit but if your 'net' profit is low you'd be wasting your time.

After you've got going and things seem to be running ok, it's easy to let a lot of hidden overheads slip through the net without noticing them. This can often make the difference between success and failure!

Keep Impeccable Accounts

The first step to keeping your overheads low is to keep impeccable accounts. As well as business accounts I keep records of every penny that I spend. I know exactly what I've spent on everything. You would be utterly amazed at what you waste money on. Keeping good records makes you aware enough to be able to eliminate the unnecessary - and this is nothing to do with being tight fisted - knowledge is power!

When I had my first sign business before I developed good record keeping habits, I was checking through my accounts and noticed that I was paying my banks and accountant a total of £3,000 per year (in dribs and drabs). I was stunned. After realizing this I changed all my bank accounts to non fee paying accounts, sacked the accountant (he only used to copy and submit what I told him anyway) and pocketed the savings which was enough to pay my mortgage at the time.

If you go to your bank and tell them that you are starting a business and open a business account, they will be delighted and will screw you accordingly. If you want a separate account for business purposes, do so, but keep it as a non fee paying personal account. Your bank doesn't need to know that you're in business!

The only downside is that people will have to make cheques out in your name (not any company name that you might have), but I found this no problem at all. Of course some banks will not let you do this, but I've never had a problem. The alternative is that they will charge you for every deposit and every withdrawal (as discreetly as they can).

Apart from saving you money on unnecessary wastage, keeping good accounts is imperative if you are ever unfortunate enough to have a tax 'enquiry' which happened to me in 2004. This was just about the worst thing that ever happened to me. Although I had good business accounts, at the time I didn't have records of personal spending (which is why I do now) and the taxman was hounding me about cash 'in' payments and personal cash 'out' payments. If this ever happens to me again I have the records to prove everything easily.

Remain a Sole Trader & Work from Home

Increasing the size of your business is riddled with problems. As you increase turnover it makes it more difficult to work from home, thereby increasing overheads (for premises). As you increase overheads, you will then need to further increase turnover, which then means you may need to take on staff (this is where your problems will really begin). This of course increases your overheads even more and thus the need to further increase your turnover. If you haven't already done so at this point you will need to register for VAT (more problems) and before you know it you'll need bigger premises and will have to borrow money to buy top of the range equipment in order to 'compete'.

Then you only need a small recession, the orders stop coming in, your outgoings will be more than your income, you'll be making staff redundant and be left with a long lease on a huge premises that you can't afford and you go bust! I've seen this happen to good people on numerous occasions.

Of course it might not happen like this. You might make an absolute fortune and good luck to you if you do. But in a nut shell if you can remain a sole trader working from home you can compete very favourably with the 'big boys' (as you won't have their overheads) and make a good 'net' profit without the fear of going bust.

Keep borrowing to the absolute minimum

I know this is easier to say than do, but remember that the charges on everything that you borrow are coming off your net profit - out of your pocket!

In some cases borrowing can improve things tremendously, but make sure that it actually does and that you borrow from the best source at the lowest interest rate over the shortest period that you can manage.

Before I bought my first graphic machine I was paying out £500 per month to buy in lettering. So buying the machine (over a 12 month period) made me only a little worse off for the first year, but considerably better off after that. At that time this was an £8,000 investment for a similar machine that is now available for less than £300!

Avoid bad debts

For some inexplicable reason it seems to be the norm that when traders purchase from you, they have at least 30 days to pay. I have never played this game. My accountant told me that I would never get away with it, but I always have.

I do business on a 'payment on collection/delivery' basis only, otherwise I'm not interested. You would be wise to follow suit. Sure, I've lost a few orders doing this, but I've NEVER been ripped off.

It only takes one company at the top of the 'borrowing chain' to go bust and the rest come tumbling down with them. I've seen it happen on numerous occasions.

But I've also always worked it the other way as well. All supplies that I purchase I pay for as I collect them (even though I have been offered credit terms many times). As a result of this I gained the respect of all my suppliers who are always happy to do business with me at very preferential rates.

Advertising

Advertising is (or should be) without doubt your most expensive overhead. The more you spend on successful advertising, the more you will increase your turnover (and hopefully your net profit). This is one overhead expense that can't be skimped on, although money spent on ineffective advertising is obviously pointless (and costly).

The direction that you wish your business to take will determine which type of advertising is most suitable. Basically you have the following choices:

    a) to aim at any trade but none in particular;

    b) to specialise in a particular trade only;

    c) to aim at vehicle graphics etc. for the general public; or

    d) a combination of these.

Word of Mouth

Personal recommendations have got to be your best (and cheapest) form of advertising, and this is without doubt how I secured most of my business. Naturally it takes time for this to 'kick in', so you can't rely on this entirely (especially in the beginning). And remember that this also works the other way round; if you generate a reputation for unreliability or poor work, the word will spread!

Your own Signs

If you are running a sign business, you would look pretty silly if you didn't have a sign of your own! Either lettering up your vehicle or using magnetic signs would do the job and is very effective (and low cost) advertising. I recommend for your own signs that you use 'reflective' material, which is five times the cost of non reflective, but the effect in the dark is stunning.

Yellow Pages

This has got to be worthwhile if you are aiming at businesses in general, but not if you are aiming at a particular trade. As they are only published once a year, it can take several months for this to become effective, so in the initial stages you will have to look at something else. I've personally never used Yellow Pages with regards to signs, but have for another business very successfully.

Direct Mail

If you are aiming at a particular trade (as I have done) this can be extremely effective, as you are able to target exactly the areas and trades that you want. I started my first sign business this way, but to keep costs down I designed and litho printed all of my own brochures/price lists, copied and typed the mailing list (from Yellow Pages in my local library) and stuffed all my own envelopes (with a little help from my friends). At the time there was a special offer on at the Post Office where I got about 5,000 mailed free.

The result was superb, but it was very hard work. After this initial special offer I was overrun with business so I then changed my advertising to Trade Magazines.

Mailing lists can be purchased from www.hilitedms.co.uk.

Trade Magazines

Just about every trade has their own magazine(s) that are only available to them via trade organizations (usually given freely).

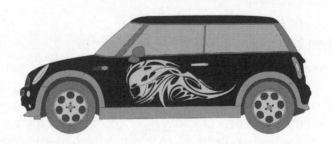

Again if you are aiming at a particular trade, this can be an extremely cost effective way of advertising. The main advantage being that the circulation will be quite low (as they will only be aimed at a particular trade), which means that you could get a half or quarter page advert relatively inexpensively. However, do check 'circulation' figures (NOT 'readership' figures) as some magazines offer far better value than others.

Unlike Yellow Pages, you could have a virtually immediate response from this type of advertising, which generally gets better after repeated insertions.

One very important point to remember with any magazine advert is that the top right hand part of a right hand page is BY FAR the most effective position. Don't let anyone try and kid you on otherwise. THIS IS A PROVEN FACT. If necessary, pay extra to get this position. It can make the difference between success and failure. I've only ever used this position.

Recently in Cyprus I was discussing this with a landscape gardener that I did some signs for. He was complaining about a lack of response from his advertising. After trying the 'right' position, he was stunned!

Trade Exhibitions

Again, if you are aiming at a particular trade, they periodically have trade exhibitions. These can be an excellent way of increasing business and one that I have used very successfully many times.

Shop Premises

A shop premises, as well as being a place from where you can operate your business is also an extremely effective advert and is bound to generate business. But of course this will work best if you are aiming at a variety of trades and perhaps vehicle graphics as well.

The downside is that this will increase your overheads to a very great degree (as mentioned previously), but if in the right position it could prove to be very lucrative.

You could of course use the premises for some other related business as well (laser printing perhaps).

Car Boot Sales/ Sunday Markets

If you are aiming at the general public for car/boat graphics etc., this can be a superb way of exposure, and very cost effective. You could take your equipment with you and operate it from your car battery (via a small inverter). Obviously you would need to make some sort of display showing examples of what you can do, and have books with various graphics that you could offer. Although I've never done this myself, I've seen other people do this very effectively.

Special Interest Magazines

Just about every 'special interest' has many magazines aimed at them, which could prove to be very cost effective advertising for you (if that's the area you are aiming at). It's not just cars that use graphics, boats (including canal boats); caravans and motor homes; and even light aircraft all use them (and have their own mags).

Special Interest Exhibitions

As well as having their own mags, there are periodic shows and events all over the country for just about every interest that you could think of.

We have a motor home and I've noticed that there is an Australian guy doing all the motor home exhibitions, making a very nice living selling graphics.

Website

In this day and age just about every business needs a website of some description, but do remember that in most cases you will need other advertising to direct your clients to your site.

Sure you could be found via the internet search engines and you should maximize this as much as possible, but I wouldn't rely on it too much unless you really know what you are doing or pay someone to do it for you.

Having someone design, produce and maintain your website could be expensive, especially if you choose the wrong company and even then will not guarantee that you will be found by the search engines. So my advice is that you create your own as I have done, or research any prospective design company very carefully - it's a jungle out there!

My websites were created (by me) using serif software which costs about £60 (see: http://www.serif.com). Alternatively you could use one of the free site builders: - Joomla or Wordpress. Both are excellent.

Ok mine might not be the best websites on the block, but I think you'll agree that they are more than adequate - and that's all they have to be! I'm certainly not a computer whizz, but I managed to do this without too much hassle and fairly easily.

But remember, the *'look'* of the site is nowhere near as important as the *'search-ability'* and for this you must study SEO (search engine optimisation). A super duper lights flashing, bells ringing website might look great, but if you're the only one who ever sees it, it aint gonna do you much good! And believe me there are too many companies out there who will produce this rot for you and relieve you of a fortune!

From the 'search engines' point of view a plain site with no fancy fonts or graphics is best, and will more likely be 'found' - but there's also much more to it than that.

More information about SEO can be found at http://astecweb.com. Also Google search *'free SEO'* and read up on it.

Having created your site with SEO in mind, you will then need a 'domain name' and a 'host' in order to go on line. A typical *.com* or *.co.uk* domain name costs £5 - £10 per year and can be obtained from http://www.123-reg.co.uk/ or http://heartinternet.co.uk (both good).

Then you will need your 'host'. You will have to transfer the name server to the host via the control panel in 123-reg or heartinternet to your chosen host - honestly it's not as complicated as it sounds, - or maybe it's just because I haven't got any hair left to pull out!

Beware of sites offering you a *free* domain name if you use their hosting, as there will inevitably be a *sting in the tail* and you will eventually have to pay for the name (and more) when you leave them to get hosting elsewhere. **Always buy your domain name** and retain ownership of same!

Many hosts offer you an initial low cost incentive and then screw you later in the hope that you can't cope with all the grief of changing.

If you are on a tight budget, to begin with you could use a free host such as http://000webhost.com which is also free of annoying adverts unlike most of the free hosts, but I have to say that this is not the perfect solution - just possibly a budget option to get you going.

I personally use paid hosting at http://astecweb.com, which enables me to host all my domains for one annual charge (about £40 per year) and I have to say this is far more reliable than the free option. And furthermore this allows me to keep complete control of my websites without getting ripped off as well as access to valuable help and assistance when necessary!

If you find the thought of all this totally daunting, then I can thoroughly recommend http://astecweb.com to do the whole lot for you (design, reliable hosting and effective SEO). Or if you already have a site created, then maybe just the all important SEO element. Don't be put off by the fact that they're in France; they are English and very, very good at what they do as well as being honestly and sensibly priced. They will discuss the best options with you to suit your budget and needs. And furthermore they're not VAT registered which gives you an immediate 20% saving!

Should you have a brochure or price list, you can make these into pdf files (via MS word or other software) and easily add these to your site as instant downloads. The eBook version of this book for instance is a pdf download from my site and was originally created in MS word.

So all in all a website should cost you very little and will help generate both business and profile.

Google Adwords

Google Adwords is a method whereby you can create online adverts for your website and pay on a *per click* basis. You choose how much you are prepared to pay *per click* and this could be anything from a single penny to £5.00 or more. The more you pay, the more exposure you will get - but it won't necessarily bring you orders.

Whether this method will be any good for you will obviously depend on who you are aiming your business at. I'll be honest - I can't make it worthwhile, but clearly it works for some people. It could be that I'm doing it wrong! At the time of writing this I'm still trying.

But be warned if you set this up and forget about it without *pausing* all your adverts, you could end up with a very nasty unexpected bill!

See: http://www.google.co.uk/adwords for more information.

Video

Make a free You Tube video! This can be done easily via 'windows movie maker' with a combination of text and photos/graphics which you can zoom in and out to create the illusion of movement, or of course if you are able to, you can make a 'proper' video.

This can then be incorporated into your website (and other sites) which could increase your profile and search ratings.

I have a few videos in my sites, to be honest the early ones aren't very good, but when I get round to it I'll improve them as I'm getting better at it all the time.

Look at http://www.learn-keyboard.co.uk/lullaby_video.html and http://www.deep-relaxation.co.uk/tibetan_bells_video.html for a couple of examples of mine. And remember these cost nothing to make and nothing to put onto You Tube.

Online Auction Sites

When you think of online auctions, unless you've been asleep for the last 10 years you would automatically think 'ebay'. But there are others, although with ebay being so strong most fail, but 'ebid' and 'bonanza' are holding their own and will get better if just more people used them. I hope that they survive and prosper as the ebay *monopoly* is not good.

Probably the most up and coming internet selling site is 'Gumtree', and guess who owns them - ebay! So they are clearly set to get bigger and remember it costs nothing to advertise your goods/services with them *and* hyperlink to your video (and website for a fee).

Anyway ebay or similar can be a superb media depending on what you are selling. The clear advantage of course is that you have worldwide coverage for a very low cost and it is also basically safe unless you do anything really stupid. The downside is that everyone wants everything for nothing on ebay so always set a starting price or a reserve.

Another disadvantage is that if you inadvertently infringe one of their many hugely ambiguous rules (or even if they think you might have); they could suspend you without warning. And as communicating with them is like trying to swing a pendulum in a bucket of glue, I would advise against building a business that relies on them more than 50% - remember: don't put all your eggs in one basket - especially that one!

Brochures/Price Lists

Few sign businesses bother with a price list as most jobs tend to vary to a very great extent according to what exactly is required, but for basic signage, it's quite possible to produce one and very helpful to your potential clients. A copy of my Cyprus price list is shown over the next few pages. If comparing prices however please note that the Cypriot pound (as it then was) is not the same as Sterling and the cost of supplies is also very different in Cyprus.

However, if you look at my two dedicated websites:

- http://www.martinwoodward.net/ukmagsigns and
- http://www.martinwoodward.net/locologos

you will find some fairly up-to-date workable UK prices for both signs and graphics. You may need to tweak these according to your needs, but they will provide a good starting point.

Feel free to explore the 'buy it now' buttons, they are active but you will not inadvertently buy anything unless you input your credit card details. And please note that these websites are for example only (exclusively for this guide) and none of the items are actually for sale.

But if you do manage to 'buy' anything, don't worry, I'll refund it for you.

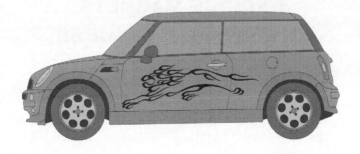

MAGNETIC & VINYL VEHICLE SIGNS FOR CARS & VANS

ALSO PRE SPACED VINYL LETTERING & FRIDGE MAGNETS
UNBEATABLE PRICES!!

Tel/Fax: 266 23239 Mobile: 99 784 158
E-mail: martinwoodward@cytanet.com.cy

MAGNETIC VEHICLE SIGNS

ON FOR BUSINESS - OFF FOR PLEASURE - INSTANTLY!

Top quality magnetic rubber, which can be fitted to any smooth steel door or side panel. Suitable for motorway use. White gloss background with up to 40 letters included in the price. Not suitable for aluminum or glass. Please measure panels carefully before ordering, remembering that magnetic signs cannot be used over *sharp* contours.

SIZES	14" (350mm)	20" (500mm)	24" (600mm)	30" (750mm)	36" (900mm)
8" (200mm)	£20.00	£25.00	£30.00	£36.00	£44.00
12" (300mm)		£36.00	£39.00	£48.00	£58.00
16" (400mm)			£51.00	£64.00	£66.00
24" (600mm)			£55.00	£69.00	£82.00

Prices are *per pair* and include up to 40 letters single colour. Add £5.00 per pair for each additional colour. Deduct 40% for single sign. No VAT applicable. Logos etc. by quotation. Phone us for alternative sizes. Add 10% p&p. Free delivery in Paphos/Polis/Pissouri.

GUARANTEED LOWEST PRICES IN CYPRUS

EXAMPLES:

SELF ADHESIVE VEHICLE SIGNS

These are the same as the magnetic signs but designed to stay on the vehicle permanently. Signs can be removed when you wish to sell the vehicle etc., but cannot be replaced.

SIZES	20" (500mm)	24" (600mm)	30" (750mm)	36" (900mm)	42" (1050mm)
8" (200mm)	£13.00	£15.00	£18.00	£22.00	£26.00
12" (300mm)	£18.00	£20.00	£25.00	£30.00	£34.00
16" (400mm)		£26.00	£33.00	£34.00	£36.00
24" (600mm)		£28.00	£35.00	£41.00	£48.00

Prices are *per pair* and include up to 40 letters single colour. Add £5.00 per pair for each additional colour. Deduct 40% for single sign. No VAT applicable. Logos etc. by quotation. Phone us for alternative sizes. Add 10% p&p. Free delivery in Paphos/Polis/Pissouri.

UK Mag-Signs Tel/Fax: 266 23239 or 99 784 158 E-mail: martinwoodward@cytanet.com.cy

PRE SPACED SELF ADHESIVE VINYL LETTERING

Available in single letters, words, sentences or cut to your requirements.
Suitable for vehicles, signs, shop windows (reversed mirror lettering available) etc.
Please note that different styles will cover different lengths

Letter Height up to	Prices	Letter Height up to	Prices
1" (25mm)	10c	7" (175mm)	68c
2" (50mm)	18c	8" (200mm)	79c
3" (75mm)	25c	9" (225mm)	89c
4" (100mm)	36c	10" (250mm)	99c
5" (125mm)	47c	11" (275mm)	£1.10
6" (150mm)	57c	12" (300mm)	£1.20

TOP QUALITY AT LOW PRICES

IMPORTANT: When ordering Vinyl Letters please state the MAXIMUM LENGTH you require the text to be, because depending on Letter Style text of the same height can be of varying length. You could find the text you have ordered may not fit the area available. If in doubt please *contact us*.

LETTER STYLES & COLOURS

HOBO - ABCDE abcde 1234
Handscript - ABCDE abcde 12345
COOPER - ABCDE abcde 12345
BATMAN ABC ABC 1234
Brush Script - ABCDE abcde 12345
VAG - ABCDE abcde 12345
BOOK ANTIQUA - ABCDE abcde
ONDINE - ABCDE abcde 12345
BOOKMAN - ABCDE abcde 12345
ARIAL NORMAL- ABCDE abcde 1235
LATIN - ABCD abcd

ARIAL BOLD- ABCDE abcde 1235
DOM BOLD - ABCDE abcde 12345
GRIZZLY BT - ABCDE abcde 12345
HUDSON ABCDE abcde 12345
SPRINT - ABCDE abcd 1234
ACCENT / ABCDE abcde
BALLOON EXTRA BOLD- ABCDE ABCDE 12345
ΩΕΡΔΣΑΠΛΚ – ΑΒΧΔΕ αβχδε
CLARENDON - ABCD abcd 12345
FORTE- ABCD abcd 12345
FLEXURE- ABCD abcd 12345

This is just a small selection of the 1000s of typestyles available.
If the style you want is not listed here, please contact us.

Colours available: BLACK, WHITE, **RED,** BLUE GREEN, YELLOW **and ORANGE**

We can also produce various 'curved' effects as below. Please phone for more details.

MAGNETIC   MAGNETIC   MAGNETIC

UK Mag-Signs Tel/Fax: 266 23239 or 99 784 158 E-mail: martinwoodward@cytanet.com.cy

RIGID SIGNS

We supply two types of rigid signs both of which are suitable for indoor and outdoor use. Corex signs are made of low cost 4mm fluted plastic and ideal for short term use i.e. Estate Agents Boards etc. 3mm Foamex signs are suitable for permanent signs i.e. Pool Rules, Warning signs etc.

CYPRUS JOY
LANDSCAPE
GARDENING SERVICES
Tel: 99 427481
E-mail: cyprusjoy@cytanet.com.cy

Corex Prices:

SIZES	12" (300mm)	18" (450mm)	24" (600mm)	30" (750mm)	36" (900mm)
12" (300mm)	£6.00	£8.00	£10.00		
18" (450mm)	£8.00	£11.00	£14.00	£17.00	£20.00
24" (600mm)	£10.00	£16.00	£18.00	£22.00	£26.00

Foamex Prices:

SIZES	12" (300mm)	18" (450mm)	24" (600mm)	30" (750mm)	36" (900mm)
12" (300mm)	£8.00	£12.00	£15.00	£18.00	£21.00
18" (450mm)	£12.00	£16.00	£20.00	£24.00	£28.00
24" (600mm)	£15.00	£20.00	£25.00	£30.00	£35.00

Prices are *per sign* and include up to 40 letters single colour. Add £3.00 per sign for each additional colour.. No VAT applicable. Logos etc. by quotation. Phone us for alternative sizes. Add 10% p&p. Free delivery in Paphos/Polis/Pissouri.

PERSONALISED FRIDGE MAGNETS

Our fridge magnets are printed onto card, laminated with rounded corners and a quarter sized piece of magnetic rubber adhered to the back.

QTY	55 x 55mm	65 x 65mm	55 x 90mm
50	£20.00	£22.50	£25.00
100	£30.00	£35.00	£40.00
200	£55.00	£65.00	£75.00

Prices include basic design, typesetting and delivery.

UK Mag-Signs Tel/Fax: 266 23239 or 99 784 158 E-mail: martinwoodward@cytanet.com.cy

Income Tax

As already mentioned keeping impeccable accounts is essential, both for your own knowledge and also for the 'taxman'.

There are many simple accounts programs on the market specifically designed for small businesses, or you could create your own using MS excel as I do. But whatever you decide the important thing is to get into the habit or imputing your entries on a daily basis at the same time as numbering and filing you receipts/invoices. This will avert a crisis at the end of the year.

Basically you need to list all of your 'income' in one section and all of you 'expenses' in another. The expenses are a little more complicated because not all of them can be claimed against tax in the same way and therefore all have to be categorised.

All of your material expenses and accountant fees etc. can be claimed 100% against tax. But other items such as your phone; motoring expenses; bank charges; heating etc. (if working from home) you will only be able to claim a percentage of depending on the amount of personal/business use. This needs to be agreed with your tax inspector. However, if you use an accountant which I certainly advise (at least for the first few years), he/she will do this for you.

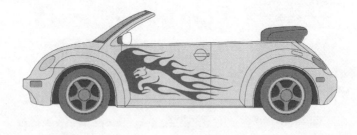

Large 'capital' items such as vehicles and machinery are also claimed differently. For these you get a reducing capital allowance each year which is adjusted so that you don't gain or lose out when you sell or right the item off. Again your accountant will do this for you. But the most important thing to remember is that your accountant can only work with the figures that you give him/her, so get into the habit of making income and expense entries on a daily basis.

VAT

VAT is dealt with by the Customs & Excise department and is completely separate from the Inland Revenue. The powers that they have to go through your affairs are no less than 'Brutal'. The threshold for compulsory VAT registration is now quite high (currently £70,000). This means that until your turnover nearly reaches that level you don't have to register, although you can register voluntarily – but don't!

If you are not registered this means that you don't charge VAT on your goods or services, but it also means that you can't claim back any of the VAT that you have to pay for materials or services that you have to purchase.

All sign material suppliers will be VAT registered and so they will obviously charge you 20% VAT on top of their quoted prices. This is something that you must remember and 'gear' into your prices. As you get to know your suppliers and if you always pay up front as I suggest, you may find that some of them will offer you discounts for cash purchases with no receipts. Obviously I would never condone such practice!

When I started my first sign business, the threshold was much lower and I had to register. Fortunately as the threshold increased I was able to de-register later. I can tell you from personal experience that there is absolutely no benefit in registering until you have to. And then you will be an unpaid tax collector which will cost you dearly in time, effort and increased accountant's fees.

Due to the pain involved I would never allow my turnover to reach the threshold level again at any cost. Believe me you don't need it! It's quite possible to earn a very good income with this business without reaching the threshold, especially if you remain a sole trader working from home.

Useful Contacts

Abel Magnets
Magnetic Panels,
Vinyls & Adhesives
www.abelmagnets.com
Tel: 0114 2495949
FIVE STAR CONTACT!

Spandex
Vinyls & Application tapes etc
www.spandex.com

Intagraph
Vinyls & Application tapes etc
http://intagraph.co.uk

Roland DG
Graphic Machines
http://www.rolanddg.com

Sign Wizard
Graphic Machines
www.signwizard.co.uk

Signmaster
Graphic Machines
http://www.signmaster.co.uk

Premier Signs
Graphic machines
Good start up offer!
www.premiersign.co.uk/offer.htm

P Cut Software
http://www.sc-x2.com

FREE WEB HOST
http://www.000webhost.com

Free corporate logos.
www.brandsoftheworld.com

Free fonts & dingbats
www.simplythebest.net/fonts

Free dingbats/fonts
www.dingbatdepot.com

Fred Cutler
Wheel Covers
www.wheelcover.com

JMC Wheel covers
www.4x4-wheel-covers.co.uk

Vinyl Corporation
Vinyls & Application Tape
www.thevinylcorporation.co.uk

List of Worldwide suppliers
www.sign-supplies.com

Application Tape Co
Vinyls & Application tapes etc
www.apptape.co.uk

Serif
Web Creation Software
www.serif.com

Gumtree
Free online advertising
www.gumtree.com

Other Books/Guides by Martin Woodward

Your Own Home Run Sign Business

Driving Instructor Training - Exposed!

A Guide to Profitable Self Employment

Magnetic Business Cards for Profit

Buy to Let on a Budget

Buying Property and Living in Cyprus

An Introduction to Traded Options

Learn How to Play Electronic Piano or Keyboard in a Week! ♪

Keyboard Improvisation One Note at a Time ♪

New Easy Original Piano / Keyboard Music
Beginners - Intermediate ♪

See: www.martinwoodward.net for details of the above

-----ooooo00000ooooo-----

See: www.deep-relaxation.co.uk for details of items below

Binaural Beat Maker Plus

The Golden Sphere

Relaxation CD's & Recordings ♪

Printed in Great Britain
by Amazon.co.uk, Ltd.,
Marston Gate.